Dumpl

Delicious Dumpling Recipes from
Around the World

Contents

Introduction 5

Asian Dumplings 6

Jiu Cai He Zi Dumplings 7

Chicken Dumpling Soup 9

Black Sesame Dumplings 11

Gyoza 13

Vegetarian dumplings 14

Rose Dumplings 15

Chinese rice dumplings – 'Zongzi' 17

Mushroom "Siu Mai" and steamed pork Dumplings 18

Chive and Prawn Potstickers 20

Prawn & Pork Dumplings 21

Beef Dumplings 23

Jian Jiao 25

Sui Kow 27

Shui Jiao 29

Caribbean Dumplings 31

Corned Beef Dumplings (Fritters) 32

Banana Dumplings (Fritters) 34

Codfish Dumplings (Fritters) 36

Sardine Dumplings 38

Callaloo Dumplings 40

Sweet Corn Dumplings 42

Flat Vegetable Dumplings 44

Puerto Rican Corn Dumplings 46

Jamaican Johnny Cakes (Fried Dumplings) 48

Trinidadian Split Pea Dumplings 50

Sweet Potato Dumplings 52

African Dumplings 53

Madombi Dumplings 54

Kaimati 56

Souskluitjies 58

North American Dumplings 60

Chicken and Cornmeal Dumplings 61

Pakistani Dumplings 63

Mantu 64

Conclusion 66

Table of Contents

Contents 2

Introduction 7

Asian Dumplings 9
- Jiu Cai He Zi Dumplings 10
- Chicken Dumpling Soup 13
- Black Sesame Dumplings 16
- Gyoza 18
- Vegetarian dumplings 20
- Rose Dumplings 22
- Chinese rice dumplings – 'Zongzi' 24
- Mushroom "Siu Mai" and steamed pork Dumplings 26
- Chive and Prawn Potstickers 28
- Prawn & Pork Dumplings 30
- Beef Dumplings 32
- Jian Jiao 34
- Sui Kow 37
- Shui Jiao 40

Caribbean Dumplings 42
- Corned Beef Dumplings (Fritters) 43
- Banana Dumplings (Fritters) 45
- Codfish Dumplings (Fritters) 47
- Sardine Dumplings 49
- Callaloo Dumplings 51
- Sweet Corn Dumplings 53
- Flat Vegetable Dumplings 55
- Puerto Rican Corn Dumplings 57
- Jamaican Johnny Cakes (Fried Dumplings) 59
- Trinidadian Split Pea Dumplings 61

Sweet Potato Dumplings 63
African Dumplings 65
　Madombi Dumplings 66
　Kaimati 68
　Souskluitjies 71
North American Dumplings 74
　Chicken and Cornmeal Dumplings 75
Pakistani Dumplings 77
　Mantu 78
Conclusion 80

Introduction

Did you know that depending on what part of the world you were raised in; the word Dumpling would have a completely different meaning to you? That's right, different world territories have their own delicious version of what a dumpling should look like as well as how it should look and taste.

In the continent of Asia, a Dumpling is known to be a dish that consists of small pieces of dough (mostly made from starch sources i.e. bread, potatoes, wonton wrappers, etc. filled with fish, sweets, meat or vegetables, then cooked. Once filled, the dumplings would be either steamed, pan fried, boiled, or even deep fried. While in other sections of the world, a dumpling is simply a starch based- side, made from flour or some other form of grain, then boiled, steamed or fried.

Regardless of where you are from, however, there are two things that will always remain the same about dumplings wherever you go, and that is that they are always delicious, and extremely easy to make, once you know what you are doing. Luckily, after taking this culinary journey with us, you will not only be equipped to successfully make these amazing dumplings that we have suggested but versatile enough also to create your own. So, without further ado, let's get started.

Asian Dumplings

Jiu Cai He Zi Dumplings

In China, a Jiu Cai He Zi is a pan-fried Chinese pancake filled with chives and scrambled eggs.

Servings: 4

Time needed: 1 ½ hours

Ingredients:

- Flour (2 cups)
- Water (1 cup, lukewarm)
- Baking Powder (3 tsp.)
- Salt (1/2 tsp for dough, 1 tsp for eggs)
- Garlic Chives (4oz, finely chopped)

- Eggs (3, beaten)
- Vermicelli (1oz., soaked and softened)
- Sesame Oil (1 tsp)
- Ground Pork (1/2 lbs., cooked)
- White Pepper (1/4 tsp)

Directions:

To create your dough, add all your dry ingredients to a large bowl, and stir with your hand until fully combined. Next gradually add water, kneading until it forms dough. NB: Your dough will be ready when it bounces back after a gentle touch. If the dough appears to be too dry then add a bit more water but be careful not to make it too sticky. Cover the dough with a plastic wrap and let stand for about 30 minutes.

In a non-stick pan over medium high heat, lightly brush it with oil and set your eggs to scramble, or create a very thinly layer of lightly fried egg with little to no color, then chop it up into thin pieces and set aside.

Next chop up your softened vermicelli noodles and chives so that they are small pieces (similar to the size of your scrambled or chopped eggs). In a medium bowl, combine your pork, vermicelli, eggs, chives, salt as well as pepper and mix until fully combined. Ensure that it is seasoned enough for your liking.

Now to assemble our dumplings: Divide your dough into 12 equal pieces and roll each piece out into a thin square. Next add 2 tablespoons of your filling mixture into the middle of each square. Fold the far end of the bottom right of the square to meet the diagonal opposite to the top left of the dough square, then repeat the same process on the opposite side. Next pinch the dumpling to seal all the openings, creating a fully pleated dumpling.

Coat lightly both sides of the dumpling with oil. Lay them on a non-stick skillet, and pour about 1/4 cup of water in the pan, set over high heat and bring to a boil. Once boiling, reduce the temperature to the medium-low and continue to cook until all the water evaporated.

Once all the water has evaporated, reduce the heat to the lowest setting and continue to cook dumplings, turning periodically until they are evenly brown on all sides. Serve and Enjoy!

Chicken Dumpling Soup

These dumplings are tasty and crunchy with every bite.

Serving: 5

Time Needed: 1½ hrs.

Ingredients:

- Wonton/ Siu Kow wrappers (20)
- Water (4 cups)

Scallion Filling:

- Mushroom- wood ear (1)
- Ground Chicken (6 oz.)

- Shrimp (4 oz., peeled and deveined)
- Water Chestnuts (2, peeled and minced)
- Green Onion (1 tablespoon, chopped)
- Seasoning
- Sesame Oil (1/2 teaspoon)
- Oil (1 ½ teaspoons)
- Shaoxing wine (1 teaspoon)
- Salt (1/2 teaspoon)
- Fish Sauce (1/2 teaspoon)
- White Pepper (1/4 tsp)
- Chicken bouillon powder (3/4 teaspoon)

Soup:

- Chicken broth (1 ¾ cups)
- Water (1 cup)
- Salt (1/4 tsp)
- Green onion (for garnish)
- White Pepper (1/4 tsp)

Directions:

Immerse mushrooms in lukewarm water for 15 minutes. Combine all the seasoning and ingredients for filling with mushroom. Mix and chill for half hour. Take a wrapper, lay it flat and fill with 1 tablespoon refrigerated filling. Wet the rim of the wrapper, fold and press to seal. Make sure it is sealed tightly. Repeat till wrappers are finished. Set dumplings aside and use a wet cloth to cover them, keeping them moist. Boil a pot of water and cook dumplings till they float, stir to avoid sticking. Take dumplings from the pot, cover to keep moist. Use another pot to heat chicken broth and water. Add pepper and salt. Put dumplings in a bowl, add soup and sprinkle with scallion. Serve hot.

Black Sesame Dumplings

You can opt to have these dumplings in plain water but to truly get the sweet dessert feeling from them, you need to have them with a natural ginger made syrup.

Serving: 4

Preparation Time: 40 minutes

Ingredients:

- Glutinous rice flour (8oz)
- Water (3/4 cup)

- Black sesame seeds (1/4 cup)
- Sugar (1/4 cup)
- Butter-unsalted (1/4 cup)
- -Ginger Syrup (1/4 tsp)
- Water (5 cups)
- Sugar (1 cup)
- Ginger (4 oz.)
- Screwpine leaves (2, optional)

Directions:

Toast seeds over a medium fire until the sesame seeds become scented. Make sure you cover the pan used as seeds may burst. Remove from flame when seeds get aromatic. Use a processor to combine seeds till they become fine. Put seeds into the pan and add butter as well as sugar, combine to make a paste. Add more butter if needed; put into a container and refrigerate. Mix flour with water and mix into a smooth paste. The paste should not stick to your hands. Divide into 16 balls. Make each ball flat and take a few seeds, using chopsticks to place into a paste. Pick up edges and pull together, then roll balls as smoothly as you can. Repeat till all paste is used up. Make ginger syrup by adding ginger and sugar to 5 cups of boiling water. Boil until water has been condensed by 1 cup, you may add more sugar if so desired. Using another pot, put some water to boil and plunge dumplings into the water. As soon as they drift to the top of the water, remove from the pot into syrup. Remove syrup from the flame and serve.

Gyoza

This is a pork based dim sum recipe having garlic and chili flavors.

Serve: 10

Time needed: 25 minutes

Ingredients:

- Ground pork: 1 lb
- Green cabbage chopped: 1 lb
- Ginger & garlic: 2 tbsp. each
- Soy sauce: ¼ cup
- Sugar: 1 tbsp.

- Wonton wrappers: 2 packages
- Vegetable oil: 1 tsp
- Gyoza: 12
- Hot water
- Basic dipping sauce
- For dipping sauce:
- Soy sauce: 2 tbsp.
- Rice wine vinegar: 1 tbsp.
- Sesame oil: ¼ tsp

Directions

Take a bowl and mix pork, garlic, cabbage, soy sauce, ginger and sugar. Fry the patty made from this into the pan with seasoning. Brush wonton skin with water and put into meat mixture in center, fold and seal the skin into half moon shape. Make rest of dumplings, then cover and refrigerate for an hour. Take a skillet and brown gyoza in heated oil for few minutes. Add hot water to cover dumplings and cook for 7 minutes. Serve with dipping sauce made by combining dipping sauce ingredients.

Vegetarian dumplings

If you want some classic vegetarian dumpling recipe, try this amazing combo of mushrooms and other vegetables.

Serve: 6

Time needed: 1 hour 15 minutes

Ingredients:

- Olive oil: 3 tbsp.
- Chopped mushrooms: 1 lb
- Chopped garlic: 4 cloves
- Grated carrot: ½ cup
- Soy sauce: 1 tbsp.
- Sesame oil: 2 tbsp.
- Sriracha: 1 tsp

- Black pepper: ½ tsp
- Green onion, sliced: 1

Directions:

Take a skillet and heat oil. Cook garlic and mushrooms for 10 minutes. Stir in cabbage and carrots and cook for 2 minutes. Remove from heat, and then add sesame oil, soy sauce, green onion and pepper. Put filling into wrappers and shape, then seal in a half moon shape. Cover dumplings with tower and refrigerate for an hour. Take a skillet and heat 1 tbsp. vegetable oil on medium heat. Fry dumplings for 4 minutes. Then add water and reduce heat. Cover and cook for 3 minutes. Serve with soy sauce.

Rose Dumplings

It's a traditional recipe in Chinese cuisine and served in breakfast and lunch mostly. It's refreshing and yummy.

Serve: 8

Time needed: 25 minutes

Ingredients:

- Flour: 2 cups
- Egg: 1
- Roses: 8
- Carrot: ½
- Mushrooms: 2

- Diced wood ear: 1 piece
- Oyster sauce: 1 tbsp.
- Dry tofu: 1 cup
- Soy sauce: 1 tbsp.
- Olive oil: 1 tsp
- Ginger root: 1

Directions:

Take a pot, mix lukewarm water with wood wear, tofu and mushrooms. Let them soak. Take another bowl, mix flour and corn flour with water. Knead dough for 20 minutes, chop carrots and soaked ingredients. Beat eggs in a bowl and mix all these fillings in a single bowl. Make dumplings out of dough and shape these into a triangle. Leave a little hole in mid to decorate with rose. Steam dumplings in boiling water steamer for 20 minutes.

Chinese rice dumplings – 'Zongzi'

This recipe has been made with glutinous rice stuffed with different fillings.

Serve: 6

Time needed: 1 hr 10 minutes

Ingredients:

- Glutinous Rice: ½ lb
- Chinese dates: 1-2 oz.
- Bamboo leaves
- Cotton thread

Directions:

Wash bamboo leaves and soak both leaves and rice overnight. Drain before using. Fold two leaves in a funnel shape and put rice in the bottom. Then add in Chinese dates and again cover with rice. Fold down leaves and seal with thread. Take a pot and boil water with Zongzi (rice dumplings) for an hour on medium heat. Serve.

Mushroom "Siu Mai" and steamed pork Dumplings

This is one of the classical dim sum creations, with sharp flavors of spices and mixture of prawn with mushrooms.

Serve: 10

Time needed: 35 minutes

Ingredients:

- Ground pork: 115 g
- Shiitake mushrooms chopped: 3
- Spring onion, chopped: 1
- Grated Ginger: 1 tbsp.

- Soy sauce: 1 tbsp.
- Shaohsing rice wine: 1 tbsp.
- Sesame oil: 1 tbsp.
- Sea salt & pepper
- Corn flour: 2 tsp
- Dumpling wrappers: 10
- Goji berries: 15
- Vegetable oil: tbsp.

Directions:

Take a bowl and mix all filling ingredients. Put some filling in mid of dumpling wrapper, shape and seal wrapper into a ball shape. Heat oil in a bamboo steamer bottom and place parchment paper. Arrange dumplings in steamer, then cover and cook for 8 minutes.

Chive and Prawn Potstickers

This is a refreshing fried dumpling to enjoy, giving an amazing combination of prawns and chive.

Serve: 4

Time needed: 40 minutes

Ingredients:

- Shrimps, peeled and minced: 2 cups
- Chinese chives: chopped: 3 tbsp.

- Oyster sauce: 1 tbsp.
- Shaohsing rice wine: 1 tbsp.
- Sea salt & white pepper
- Dumpling wrappers: 30
- Peanut oil: 2 tbsp.
- Corn flour

Directions:

Take a bowl and mix all filling ingredients. Put some corn flour in a tray. Have a dumpling wrapper in your palm and put some filling; press and seal wrapper in a half moon shape. Put all pot stickers this way. Take a skillet and heat oil. Cook for 5 to 7 minutes. Then add water till edges of skillet. Cover and cook for another 10 minutes. Serve and enjoy.

Prawn & Pork Dumplings

Get this unique combo of pork and prawns, filled with interesting and new flavors.

Serve: 8

Time needed: 35 minutes

Ingredients:

- Ground pork: 15 g
- Raw prawns, coarsely diced: 115 g
- Spring Onion chopped: 1
- Grated Ginger: 1 tbsp.
- Soy sauce: 1 tbsp.+ 2 tbsp.
- Rice wine: 1 tbsp.
- Corn flour: 2 tbsp.

- Sesame oil: 1 tsp
- Sea salt & black pepper
- Dumpling wrappers: 10
- Chili sauce: 1 tbsp.

Directions:

Take a bowl and mix onion, ginger, prawns, pork, soy sauce, rice wine, salt, pepper, corn flour, and sesame oil. Take a dumpling wrapper and put in fillings. Shape and seal the wrapper into half moon shape. Heat oil in a bamboo steamer bottom and place parchment paper. Arrange dumplings in steamer, then cover and cook for 8 minutes. Serve with chili sauce and soy sauce dip.

Beef Dumplings

Ground Beef go great in these dumplings too.

Serve: 8

Time needed: 35 minutes

Ingredients:

- Ground beef: 15 g
- Spring Onion chopped: 1
- Ginger powder: 1 tbsp.
- Soy sauce: 1 tbsp. + 2 tbsp.
- Rice wine: 1 tbsp.
- Corn flour: 2 tbsp.
- Sesame oil: 1 tsp
- Sea salt & black pepper

- Dumpling wrappers: 10
- Chili sauce: 1 tbsp.

Directions:

Take a bowl and mix onion, ginger powder, beef, soy sauce, rice wine, salt and pepper, corn flour and sesame oil. Take a dumpling wrapper and put in fillings. Shape and seal the wrapper into half moon shape. Heat oil in a bamboo steamer bottom and place parchment paper. Arrange dumplings in steamer, then cover and cook for 8 minutes. Serve with chili sauce and soy sauce dip.

Jian Jiao

Jian Jiao is a pan-fried dumpling, usually made from eggs cooked into an omelette with meat filling inside, which is usually served during Chinese New Year.

Serving: 6-8

Time needed: 1 hour

Ingredients:

Filling:

- ½ cup of ground chicken
- 1 tbsp. of Shaoxing wine
- 1 pinch of salt
- 2 stalks of finely diced spring onion

- 1 pinch of white pepper
- 1/2 tbsp. of sesame oil.

Dumpling Wrapper:

- 4 eggs
- 1 tbsp. of corn starch
- 1/2 tbsp. of water.
- Sauce:
- 2 tbsp. of soy sauce
- 1tbsp. of Shaoxing wine
- 2 cups of water
- 1 pinch of salt and sugar
- 1 tbsp. of water
- 1 tbsp. of corn starch.

Directions

For filling, mix all the ingredients together and set aside for 30minutes.

Beat the eggs and mix the water and cornstarch. Preheat a non-stick pan with some oil. Add 1 tbsp. of the egg mixture and disperse it on the pan with a spoon to form a circular shape of about 3-inch. Ensure the egg mixture is "thick" enough to do this.

When the bottom is cooked, and the top is still wet, add about one tsp of the filling in the middle of the egg, and then bend/fold the egg over it; tightly press the edges gently, so it seals. A half circle is formed at this stage. Uncooked the filling at this point and repeat until you are done with the eggs and filling.

Put the sauce ingredients (except for cornstarch mixture) in a medium size pot with a lid and bring it to boil. You can have a taste and adjust to your liking and then add the egg dumplings made above. Reduce the heat and cover, then cook it gently for 15 minutes. Next, add your cornstarch mixture, then bring it back to boil, stirring till it gets thickened. Turn off the heat and serve immediately.

Sui Kow

This recipe marries shrimp, oyster sauce and pork together in one delicious dumpling.

Serves: 12

Time needed: 1 Hour

Ingredients:

- 160g medium size shrimps
- 80g semi-lean pork (minced)
- 1 tablespoon of coriander leaves (use the leaves only and must be finely diced)
- 25 pieces of round-shaped dumpling wrappers
- 3 pieces of water chestnuts
- 30g carrots

- 2 pieces of dried mushrooms
- water for boiling
- 1 handful of diced spring onions
- 1 handful of frozen green peas

Seasonings:

- 2 tablespoons of oyster sauce
- 2 teaspoons of corn starch
- 1 teaspoon of sesame oil
- 1 teaspoon of cooking oil
- 1 teaspoon of salt,
- 1 teaspoon of sugar
- 1 dash white pepper

Directions

Filling:

Rinse the prawns, devein and peel under a running tap, then dry with a kitchen towel. Split them into 2 equal portions. In the 1st portion – put 1 shrimp on a chopping board and smash hit to flatten it. Repeat the same method for all the shrimps. Chop the shrimps with the back of a chopper till it is fine and sticky. Beat lightly till a paste is formed. In the 2nd portion – it is chopped roughly into smaller chunks. Now, wash and soak the mushrooms in water to get softer, then drain and squeeze dry. Next chop your water chestnuts, carrots, and soaked mushrooms into fine cubes.

Combine the seasoning and all the ingredients- (prawns, pork, water chestnuts, carrots, mushrooms, green peas, coriander leaves- in a large mixing bowl and stir in one direction until it is well mixed. Cover the bowl with a wrap and set aside in the refrigerator to cool for at least an hour.

Wrapping & Cooking

Prepare a clean cloth to wipe, clean and dry your hands. Place the dumpling wrapper on your palm and put one tsp of filling in the center of the wrapper. Wet the wrapper's edge, fold it in half and seal by pressing firmly. Transfer it to a tray dusted with flour to avoid them from sticking and fill it to two-third level in a large pot with water and boil. The dumplings are divided into two batches and placed beside each other. Stir in a clockwise direction to prevent the dumplings from sticking together.

Boil again and reduce the heat to low to keep cooking (without cover) with medium heat and allow it to boil again. Repeat the process until the filling is cooked, so as to prevent the wrapper from breaking and make the cooked filling tenderer. Turn off the heat when the dumpling is cooked and place them in a serving bowl with sesame oil sprinkled on it. Pour some broth over the dumplings and garnish with the diced spring onion and dash of white pepper powder. Then, serve immediately

Cook's Notes: The Dumpling is cooked thoroughly when the dumpling wrapper has become transparent and expanded slightly, the prawns appear slightly pink, and the dumplings float on the surface of the water.

Shui Jiao

Light and delicious dumplings generally served in soups.

Serves: 10

Time needed: 1 ½ hour

Ingredients:

- Sesame Oil (4 tbsp. & 1 tsp.)
- Soy Sauce (4 tbsp.)
- Black Vinegar (2 tbsp.)
- Garlic (3½ oz.)
- Scallions (1½ cups, finely chopped)
- Mushroom powder (2 tsp.)
- Corn Starch (1 tsp.)
- Salt (1 tsp.)

- Ginger (1/2 tsp., grated)
- Black Pepper (½ tsp.)
- Wonton wrappers (30, 4 ½ inch, round)
- Pork (1 lb., ground)

Directions

In a small bowl, mix together 1 teaspoon of soy sauce, vinegar and sesame oil, then set aside. Next prepare a baking sheet by adding a parchment paper to it and sprinkling it with flour. Also set aside a baking sheet with parchment paper and sprinkle it with flour. Combine all your remaining ingredients in a large bowl and stir forcefully to combine.

Next, assemble your dumplings by adding a tablespoon of pork filling onto the middle of the wrapper, rubbing water on the other edges of the wrapper, then folding it in half with a damp cloth, while you work on the remaining dumplings.

Set a pot of water on to boil and add salt to taste. Once boiling, add your dumpling in and allow to cook on medium heat until fully cooked (about 8 minutes). Serve with sesame oil sauce that you set aside earlier and enjoy.

Caribbean Dumplings

Corned Beef Dumplings (Fritters)

Corned beef fritters are Caribbean-flavored dumplings that will be a hit with anyone who has a taste for them. Be careful when adding salt to this recipe as canned corned beef can be quite salty.

Serves: 4

Preparation Time: 35 minutes

Ingredients:

- Flour (1 cup)
- Egg (1)
- Butter (1 tablespoon, melted)
- Black pepper
- Baking powder (1 teaspoon)

- Milk (1/2 cup)
- Oil (for frying)
- Salt (1 tsp.)
- Onion (1, grated)
- Herbs (1/4 cup, diced, fresh)
- Potatoes (2 peeled and shredded)
- Corned Beef (8 oz., canned)

Directions:

Heat oil in a skillet and add onions, sauté for 2 minutes, then add potatoes and herbs. Stir and cook for 3 minutes, then remove from heat. Heat some oil for frying. Sift dry ingredients into a bowl; beat egg and add butter and milk. Add wet mixture to the dry and mix together until thoroughly combined, then add potatoes and corned beef. Spoon drops of the mixture into oil and fry until golden. Remove from oil and place on paper towels to remove excess oil. Serve and enjoy!

Banana Dumplings (Fritters)

These are Caribbean specialty and are favorite among children. You could even pair these with some ice cream and serve it as a dessert.

Serves: 4

Preparation Time: 35 minutes

Ingredients

- Flour (1 cup)
- Egg (1)
- Butter (1 tablespoon, melted)
- Baking powder (1 teaspoon)
- Milk (1/2 cup)

- Oil (for frying)
- Salt (1 tsp.)
- Sugar (2 tablespoons)
- Banana (1 cup, mashed)
- Cinnamon (1/2 teaspoon)

Directions:

Heat oil in a skillet, sift dry ingredients into a bowl, beat egg, and add butter and milk. Add wet mixture to the dry and mix together until thoroughly combined, then add banana and stir to combine. Spoon drops of the mixture into oil and fry until golden. Remove from oil and place on paper towels to remove excess oil. Serve and enjoy!

Codfish Dumplings (Fritters)

These codfish dumplings are Caribbean favorite and you won't believe just how good they are. These are usually had around breakfast time with a cup of cocoa tea.

Serves: 4

Preparation Time: 35 minutes

Ingredients:

- Flour (1 cup)
- Cilantro (2 tablespoons, chopped)
- Codfish (1/2 lb)
- Butter (1 tablespoon, melted)
- Black pepper (1 teaspoon)

- Baking powder (2 teaspoons)
- Water (1/2 cup)
- Oil (for frying)
- Salt (1 teaspoon)
- Garlic (1 clove, diced)
- Green onion (1 teaspoon)

Directions:

Heat water in a small saucepan and place codfish into it. Boil for 15 minutes, remove from pan and place in cold water. When cooled, remove bones and skin and break into pieces. Heat oil in a skillet. Put all remaining ingredients into a bowl and mix together to combine; add codfish and stir. Spoon drops of the mixture into oil and fry until golden. Remove from oil and place on paper towels to remove excess oil. Serve and enjoy.

Sardine Dumplings

If you love sardines, you will love these dumplings.

Serves: 4

Time needed: 35 minutes

Ingredients:

- Flour (1 cup)
- Cilantro (2 tablespoons, chopped)
- Sardines (3 cans, drained and crushed)
- Butter (1 tablespoon, melted)
- Black pepper (1 tsp.)
- Baking powder (2 teaspoons)

- Water (1/2 cup)
- Oil (for frying)
- Salt (1 tsp.)
- Garlic (1 clove, diced)
- Green onion (2 teaspoons)

Directions:

Add all your ingredients into a bowl and mix together to combine. Spoon drops of the mixture into oil and fry until golden. Remove from oil and place on paper towels to remove excess oil. Serve and enjoy.

Callaloo Dumplings

Tasty vegetarian Caribbean dumpling.

Serves: 4

Time needed: 35 minutes

Ingredients:

- Flour (1 cup)
- Cilantro (2 tablespoons, chopped)
- Callaloo (1 bunch, washed and chopped)
- Butter (1 tablespoon, melted)
- Black pepper (1 tsp.)
- Baking powder (2 teaspoons)
- Water (1/2 cup)
- Oil (for frying)

- Salt (1 tsp.)
- Garlic (1 clove, diced)
- Green onion (2teaspoons)

Directions:

Add all your ingredients into a bowl and mix together to combine. Spoon drops of the mixture into oil and fry until golden. Remove from oil and place on paper towels to remove excess oil. Serve and enjoy.

Sweet Corn Dumplings

This recipe makes the perfect appetizer or snack.

Serves: 4

Time needed: 35 minutes

Ingredients:

- Flour (1 cup)
- Cornmeal (1/2 cup)
- Sugar (3 tablespoons)
- Butter (1 tablespoon, melted)
- Black pepper (1 teaspoons)
- Baking powder (2 teaspoons)
- Water (1/2 cup)

- Oil (for frying)
- Salt (1 tsp.)
- Garlic (1 clove, diced)
- Green onion (2teaspoons)

Directions:

Add all your ingredients into a bowl and mix together to combine. Spoon drops of the mixture into oil and fry until golden. Remove from oil and place on paper towels to remove excess oil. Serve and enjoy.

Flat Vegetable Dumplings

When it comes to vegetable dumplings, you really can get in as much variety as you choose. You can mix and match your favorite veggies to create the best fritters for your taste.

Serves: 4

Preparation Time: 35 minutes

Ingredients:

- Flour (1 cup)
- Egg (1)
- Butter (1 tablespoon, melted)
- Black pepper
- Baking powder (1 teaspoon)
- Milk (1/2 cup)
- Oil (1 tbsp.)
- Salt (¼ tbsp.)
- Herbs (1/4 cup, diced, fresh)
- Carrots (1/4 cup, shredded)
- Cabbage (1/4 cup, shredded)
- Onions (1/2, chopped)

Directions:

Heat oil in a skillet and add onions. Sauté for 2 minutes then add carrots, cabbage, and fresh herbs. Stir and cook for 3 minutes, then remove from heat. Heat some oil for frying. Sift dry ingredients into a bowl; beat egg and add butter and milk. Add wet mixture to the dry and mix together until thoroughly combined, then add stir fried vegetables and stir. Spoon drops of the mixture into oil and fry until golden. Remove from oil and place on paper towels to remove excess oil. Serve and enjoy!

Puerto Rican Corn Dumplings

This Puerto Rican style corn dumpling is crunchy on the outside and buttery sweet on the inside. Can be served with a variety of meals or as a snack.

Serves: 6

Time needed: 30 minutes

Ingredients:

- 6 oz. of cornmeal
- 10 tsp. of granulated sugar
- 3 tsp. of butter
- 1 tsp. of salt
- 1 ½ pt. of vegetable oil

- 1 pt. of water
- 8 tbsp. of mayonnaise
- 4 tbsp. of ketchup
- ¼ tsp. of garlic salt (optional)
- 2 tsp. of oil (additional)

Directions:

Boil water, stir in salt, sugar and butter until sugar has totally dissolved. Lower flame, whisk in 4 ounces of cornmeal until it is a smooth paste. Stir in additional two ounces to make a very stiff dough. Heat one and a half pint of oil in a saucepan or deep fryer until extremely hot. Grease palm properly with some oil. Scoop a small piece of cornmeal dough. Roll it into a circle, then roll and shape them into a 3-inch-long stick. Deep fry until golden brown. Drain on a napkin and keep warm. Combine ketchup, mayonnaise and garlic salt, then stir thoroughly. Serve as a dipping sauce with cornmeal sticks.

Jamaican Johnny Cakes (Fried Dumplings)

If you have ever been to Jamaica, you would realize that there are certain specialties that are common in every household, and this recipe provides **Directions** for one such staple… Jamaican fried dumplings.

Serves: 7

Time needed: 30 minutes

Ingredients:

- Canola Oil (enough for deep frying)
- All-Purpose Flour (2 cups)
- Baking Powder (1 tbsp.)
- Sugar (1½ tbsp.)

- Salt (¼ tsp.)
- Butter (2 tbsp.)
- Milk (1/3 cup)

Directions:

First, set your oil on to heat up to 325 degrees over medium-high heat. While oil is heating, start preparing your dumpling dough by combining all your dry ingredients in a large bowl. Next, add your butter to the flour mixture and use your hand to crumble the butter in the flour. Then add your milk and knead to form a smooth dough. Divide your dough into 7 even pieces and roll each piece into a ball. Once your oil has reached the required temperature, carefully drop the dough balls into the oils and fry until golden brown on all sides (should be about 5-8 minutes. Drain excess oil from dumplings, using a paper towel then serve and enjoy!

Trinidadian Split Pea Dumplings

This recipe is great for a classic Trini snack.

Serves: 12

Time needed: 30 minutes

Ingredients:

- Split peas (1 cup, yellow, soaked)
- Onion (1, finely chopped)
- Garlic (4 cloves, minced)
- Cilantro (2 tablespoons, finely chopped)
- Turmeric (1/2 tsp, ground)
- Cumin (1/4 tsp., ground)
- Paprika (1/4 tsp., ground)
- Cayenne Pepper (1/4 tsp., ground)
- Salt (1 tsp.)
- Oil (for frying)

Directions:

Add your soaked split peas to a food processor and pulse until it becomes a paste. Transfer your paste to a large bowl and add the remaining ingredients and mix until fully combined. Separate into 12 even portions and form each portion into a ball. Set your oil in a skillet, over medium heat and once hot, fry your dumplings until fully golden brown (about 4 minutes). Cool slightly and serve.

Sweet Potato Dumplings

This recipe is great for vegetarians and meat lovers alike.

Serves: 12

Time needed: 30 minutes

Ingredients:

- Sweet Potato (2lbs., peeled, cooked)
- Onion (1, finely chopped)
- Garlic (4 cloves, minced)
- Cilantro (2 tablespoons, finely chopped)
- Paprika (1/4 teaspoon., ground)
- Black Pepper (1/4 teaspoon., ground)
- Salt (1 teaspoon.)

- Oil (for frying)

Directions:

Add your sweet potato to a food processor and pulse until it becomes a paste. Transfer your paste to a large bowl, add the remaining ingredients and mix until fully combined. Separate into 12 even portions and form each portion into a ball. Set your oil in a skillet, over medium heat and once hot, fry your dumplings until fully golden brown (about 4 minutes). Cool slightly and serve.

African Dumplings

Madombi Dumplings

Madombi is a delicious side dish, popular in Botswana.

Serves: 4

Time needed: 1hr

Ingredients:

- All-Purpose Flour (500g)
- Yeast (2 tbsp.)
- Water (1 cup, lukewarm)
- Flour (50 g, for dusting)

- Oil (1 tbsp.)
- Water (1 cup, for cooking)

Directions:

To begin, sift your flour and yeast into a bowl. Next add your water gradually while kneading to form dough. NB: It is important that you only add enough water to form a smooth dough. Continue to knead dough for about 5 minutes. Cover with a damp cloth and set aside to proof for about 30 minutes. Next, divide the dough into 4 equal pieces and form each piece into a ball. In a large non-stick pot, add your oil over high heat along with 1 cup of water, and allow to come to a boil. Once the water begins to boil, carefully add your dumplings so that they are not touching each other and lower the heat to medium. Allow the dumplings to cook for about 20 minutes. NB: Be sure to frequently check on the dumplings while cooking as the water will be evaporating. If the water fully evaporates before your 20 minutes are done, then add another ½ cup of hot water. Serve and enjoy.

Kaimati

This recipe takes us over to Kenya with their famous sweet dumplings. These are perfect for an appetizer or just a semi-sweet snack.

Serves: 12

Time needed: 2hrs 30min

Ingredients:

Dumplings:

- All purpose flour (1 cup)
- Yogurt (1/2 cup, plain)
- Water (1/2 cup)
- Yeast (1 tsp., instant)
- Sugar (1 tsp.)
- Cinnamon Powder (1 tsp.)
- Vegetable oil (2 cups, for frying)
- Syrup
- Sugar (1 cup)
- Water (1 cup)
- Cardamom (2 tbsp.)
- Lemon Juice (1 tbsp.)
- Lemon Zest (1 tbsp.)

Directions

To create your dumpling dough, add all your ingredients in a mixer with a dough hook and mix to form a sticky dough. Cover and let rest for 2 hours. While your dough is resting, prepare your syrup by adding your sugar and water to a saucepan and bringing it to a boil. Lower the heat and continue to cook until all the sugar has dissolved. Once all the sugar has dissolved, add in your remaining ingredients and simmer until the syrup easily coasts the back of a spoon (about 6 – 8 minutes). Set aside to cool down.

Now let's cook our dumplings: Set your vegetable oil in a wok over medium heat to get hot. Once hot, use a spoon or an ice cream scoop to drop even sized dough balls into the hot oil, then fry until completely golden. Drain the excess oil and coat in syrup for up to a minute. NB: The longer you soak the dumplings in the syrup, the sweeter they will become. Serve and enjoy.

Souskluitjies

Souskluitjies or Cinnamon Dumplings is a popular dessert dumpling, generally served in South Africa.

Serves: 12

time needed: 30 minutes

Ingredients:

For Dumpling:

- White Flour (250g)
- Baking Powder (25g)
- Butter (25g, softened)

- Eggs (3)
- Milk (125ml)
- Salt (1/2 tsp, to taste)

For Sauce:

- Water (1.25L)
- Sugar (750g)
- Salt (1g)
- Vinegar (25ml)
- Butter (25ml, melted)
- Cinnamon (25g, ground)
- Cloves (1 tsp., ground)
- Sherry (125ml)
- Custard Powder (2 tbsp.)

Directions

Create the dumpling batter by adding all the dumpling ingredients to a large bowl and mixing until fully incorporated. Next, set on your water and salt on to boil in a saucepan over medium heat. Once the water begins to boil, carefully dip spoonfuls of dumpling batter into the water. Cover the pan and allow dumpling to cook undisturbed for 10 minutes. Once the dumplings are done, remove them from the water, using a slotted spoon and set aside. Next, add the remaining sauce ingredients, except your custard powder to the same pot of water that you just took the dumplings from and cook until the sugar completely dissolves. While waiting, mix your custard powder together with 3 – 4 tablespoons of cold water to create a paste. Slowly add your custard paste to the pot, stirring as the syrup thickens. Pour your hot syrup over your dumplings. Serve and enjoy.

North American Dumplings

Chicken and Cornmeal Dumplings

This one pot meal is full of protein and is bursting with flavor. These homemade dumplings are filling and pair deliciously with the chicken. Get that slow cooker out and try this wonderful meal.

Serves: 2

Preparation Time: 4-6 hours

Ingredients:

- Carrots (2, sliced thin)
- Corn kernels (1/3 cup)
- Garlic (2 cloves, diced)
- Black pepper (1/4 teaspoon)
- Chicken broth (1 cup, low salt)

- Flour (1 tablespoon)
- Celery (1 stalk, sliced thin)
- Onion (1/2, sliced thin)
- Rosemary (1 teaspoon)
- Chicken thighs (2, skin removed)
- Milk (1/2 cup, fat-free)

For dumplings:

- Flour (1/4 cup)
- Baking powder (1/2 teaspoon)
- Egg white (1)
- Canola oil (1 tablespoon)
- Cornmeal (1/4 cup)
- Salt (1/4 tsp.)
- Milk (1 tablespoon, fat-free)

Directions:

Prepare dumplings by combining flour, baking powder, salt and cornmeal in a bowl. Combine milk, oil and egg white in a separate bowl. Add wet mixture to dry mix and stir to combine until moist. Add carrots, corn, garlic, black pepper, celery, onion and rosemary to slow cooker. Then put in chicken and broth. Set on low heat and cook for 7-8 hours or on high heat for 3-4 hours. Remove chicken from slow cooker and cool for 5 minutes, then remove bones and chop chicken and return to cooker. Combine flour and milk and add to slow cooker. Use a spoon to drop dumplings into the cooker. Cook for an additional 20-25 minutes. Serve hot and enjoy!

Pakistani Dumplings

Mantu

Beautiful and tasty little dumplings

Serves: 4

Time needed: 40 minutes

Ingredients:

- ¼ cup of vegetable oil or clarified butter (ghee)
- 1-pound lean minced lamb
- 2 teaspoons finely chopped garlic
- 4 onions, finely chopped
- 1 teaspoon ground cumin
- ¼ teaspoon chili powder
- ½ teaspoon ground coriander
- ½ teaspoon salt

- 40 Shanghai wonton wrappers (square white)

Preparation:

Heat the wok, adding ghee or butter to melt, add the lamb and fry on low heat and move around until it is golden brown. Add onion and still stir; you are going to notice how the onion becomes transparent. Now add salt, garlic, and all the spices, keep stirring for about 5 minutes or a little more. Get a bowl and put what you were cooking in. Put a teaspoon of lamb filling in a wonton wrapper. You are going to make a square by brushing the edges with water, and then meeting a couple of opposite corners. Also, seal the remaining edges. Repeat with the rest of the lamb filling (these are the mantu). Place them in a steamer for around 15 minutes, but make sure they do not touch. After they are done, top echo one off with yogurt, a sprinkle of parsley and Dahl.

Conclusion

There you have it; 30 Dumpling recipes from across the globe. We hope you enjoyed taking the culinary journey with us and that you learned a lot at each stop along the way. There's no need to stop cooking now. Grab another copy of our books and let's dive in a brand-new adventure. See you in the kitchen!

Made in the USA
Middletown, DE
15 March 2020